15 25

W9-BXY-829

Safe Kids
Safety at Home

Dana Meachen Rau

Marshall Cavendish
Benchmark
New York

Your home is a fun place to play.

Be safe in your home.

Always pick up after playing.

You can trip on toys on the floor.

Some toys can make babies *choke*.

Be sure to put away all the small pieces.

Do not run on the stairs in socks.

You could slip and fall.

Do not touch an *outlet*.

An outlet can give you
a shock.

Check your bath before you get in.

Hot water can burn you.

Only grown-ups should touch *medicine*.

Some medicines can make you very sick.

Many cleaners can make you sick, too.

Do not touch them!

Always cook with a grown-up.

Stoves can be very hot.

Put food back in the refrigerator.

Some foods can *spoil* and make you sick.

Be safe when you play outside, too.

Do not climb too high.

Play in your own yard.

Never talk to strangers.

Be a safe kid at home.

Be Safe

bath

cleaners

medicine

outlet

stairs

toys

yard

Challenge Words

choke (chohk) To not be able to breathe or swallow.

medicine (MED-i-sin) A drink or pill that helps you get better when you are sick.

outlet The hole in the wall for plugs.

spoil To turn rotten and unsafe to eat.

Index

Page numbers in **boldface** are illustrations.

About the Author

Dana Meachen Rau is the author of many other titles in the Bookworms series, as well as other nonfiction and early reader books. She lives in Burlington, Connecticut, with her husband and two children.

With thanks to the Reading Consultants:

Nanci Vargus, Ed.D., is an Assistant Professor of Elementary Education at the University of Indianapolis.

Beth Walker Gambro is an Adjunct Professor at the University of Saint Francis in Joliet, Illinois.

Marshall Cavendish Benchmark
99 White Plains Road
Tarrytown, New York 10591-9001
www.marshallcavendish.us

Library of Congress Cataloging-in-Publication Data

Rau, Dana Meachen, 1971-
Safety at home / by Dana Meachen Rau.
p. cm. — (Bookworms : Safe kids)
Includes index.
Summary: "Identifies common hazards in the home and advises how to deal with them"
—Provided by publisher.
ISBN 978-0-7614-4089-5
1. Home accidents—Prevention—Juvenile literature. I. Title.
TX150.R39 2009
363.13'7—dc22
2008044933

Editor: Christina Gardeski
Publisher: Michelle Bisson
Designer: Virginia Pope
Art Director: Anahid Hamparian

Photo Research by Anne Burns Images

Cover Photo by *Getty Images*/Dave & Les Jacobs

The photographs in this book are used with permission and through the courtesy of:
Getty Images: pp. 1, 11, 28BL Jeffrey Coolidge; pp. 9, 28BR Margo Silver;
pp. 15, 28TR David Buffington; pp. 25, 29R Bambu Productions. *Corbis*: p. 3 Steve Cole;
p. 19 Jose L. Pelaez; p. 23 John-Francis Bourke/zefa; p. 27 Tracy Kahn.
Alamy Images: p. 5 David R. Frazier Photolibrary; pp. 7, 29L sciencephotos;
pp. 13, 28TL Jack Sullivan; pp. 17, 28TC Chris Pancewicz. *Photo Edit, Inc.*: p. 21 Myrleen Pearson.

Printed in Malaysia
1 3 5 6 4 2